HOW TO MAKE XMAS BC

Master the Art of Making Gorgeous Christmas Bows — A Beginner's Guide to Easy, Elegant, and Festive DIY Ribbon Designs

FLETCHER KAROLINE

Table of Contents

CHAPTER ONE 4
   Introduction 4
   The Importance of Bows in Holiday Decoration 6
   Setting up Your Craft Space 8
   Essential Materials and Tools 10
   Types of Ribbons 11
   Choosing the appropriate ribbon for your project 12

CHAPTER TWO 19
   Basic Bow-Making Techniques 19
   Understanding Ribbon Properties 19
   Fundamental Folding and Looping Methods 20
   The Simple Loop Measuring Ribbon 21
   The Classic Two-Loop Bow 21
   The Multiple Loop Bow with Layering Loops 21
   Using Twists for Texture 22
   Creating Tails 22
   Securing bows with knots, wires, and adhesives 22
   Twist Ties and String for Temporary Holds 24
   Mastering Symmetry and Proportion 24
   Practice Exercises to Improve Your Skills 25

CHAPTER THREE 27
   Simple Single Loop Bow 27
   Ribbon Variations 29
   Applications for Single Loop Bows in Decor 30

CHAPTER FOUR 32
   The Classic Two-Loop Bow 32
   Techniques for Tight Centers 34
   Decorating Gift Packages 35

CHAPTER FIVE 38
   The Multi-Loop Gift Bow 38
   Layering Techniques For Depth 41

- Customizing using various ribbon widths 42
- Creative ideas: 43

CHAPTER SIX 45
- The Floral Pom-pom Bow 45
- Color and texture combinations 47
- Decoration ideas for wreaths and centerpieces include 48

CHAPTER SEVEN 52
- Wired Ribbon Bows 52
- Shaping and Sculpting Techniques 53
- Creating dynamic tree toppers 54

CHAPTER EIGHT 58
- Layered and Stacked Bows 58
- Mixing Ribbon Types and Patterns 58
- Layering Techniques 58
- Assembling Multi-Tiered Designs 59
- Adding Embellishments for Extra Flair 60
- Applications 61

CHAPTER NINE 63
- The Flower-Shaped Bow 63
- Crafting Petal and Bloom Structures 63
- Using Fabric and Ribbon Together 65

CHAPTER TEN 67
- The Star Bow 67
- Folding Techniques for Star Shapes 67
- Incorporating Metallic and Glitter Ribbons 69
- Perfecting the Star for Gift Wrapping 69
- Variations and Creative Ideas 71
- Applications beyond Gift Wrapping 71
- TUTORIAL VIDEOS 73

CHAPTER ONE

Introduction

Welcome to the World of Christmas Bow Making!

Consider a comfortable winter evening with snowflakes slowly falling outside your window, a warm glow from candles flickering softly, and the aroma of pine and cinnamon. A magnificent Christmas tree stands in the corner of your living room, its branches covered with flashing lights and sparkling ornaments. But something is missing: a personal touch that adds warmth and character to your Christmas decorations. This is where the tradition of crafting Christmas bows comes to life.

Welcome to a world where simple strands of ribbon change into stunning decorations that capture the season's essence. Whether you're an experienced crafter or just starting, this book invites you to discover the delight of creating your own Christmas bows—adding elegance, charm, and a personal touch to your holiday celebrations.

The Joy of Handmade Decorations

Handmade crafts contain a certain type of enchantment. Each bow you make is a piece of your heart, a reflection of your personality, and a story that unfolds with each loop and twist. As you weave ribbons between your fingertips, you'll realize that bow-making is more than just a skill; it's a treasured custom that brings families and friends together.

Consider the joy on a loved one's face as they unwrap a gift with a beautifully designed bow or the warmth that permeates your home as guests admire the personalized decorations you've painstakingly placed around each room. Handmade bows are more than just ornaments; they communicate the love, caring, and festive spirit that make the holiday season so wonderful.

How To Use This Book:

This book guides a creative journey through the wonderful art of bow creation. Designed with both novices and expert crafters in mind, it provides step-by-step instructions, practical advice, and inspiring ideas to help you create bows that are as unique as you.

Here's how to get the most out of this book.

Start from the Beginning: If you're new to bow manufacturing, start with the fundamental chapters, which cover key materials, tools, and basic techniques. This will give you the expertise and confidence to handle more complex designs.

Visualize with Descriptive Guidance: Because this book lacks graphics, we've taken particular care to give vivid, thorough descriptions to walk you through each step. Close your eyes and imagine the textures, colors, and movements as you read, enabling your imagination to picture the process.

Practice and Experiment: Don't be hesitant to try new ribbons, styles, and approaches. Use the practice activities to improve your skills, and keep in mind that each bow you make is an opportunity to learn.

Personalize Your Creations: Throughout the book, you'll find ideas for personalizing your bows to match your style and surroundings. Allow your originality and personality to shine through.

Refer back as needed: Use the book as a reference. Reread chapters for clarification, review skills, or for inspiration whenever you need it.

As you turn the pages, allow yourself to be lost in the joy of making. Together, we'll explore the limitless possibilities of ribbons, transforming them into stunning bows that will bring a touch of magic to your Christmas festivities.

The Importance of Bows in Holiday Decoration

Bows are the ultimate finishing touch, adding harmony and beauty to holiday decor. They are the graceful flourish on top of a nicely wrapped gift, the vivid accent that brings life to a wreath, and the playful element that lends personality to a Christmas tree.

Imagine coming into a room with garlands draped over the mantelpiece, their rich greenery entwined with shimmering lights and accented with beautiful bows. The bows have wide and circular loops, and cascading tails that gently curl and sway with the slightest breeze, and their rich hues compliment the festive palette of reds, greens, golds, and silvers. They catch the light and reflect a gentle sheen that attracts the eye in and encourages a closer look.

Bows are not simply adornment, but also statements of style and feeling. A simple burlap bow oozes rustic appeal and is ideal for a comfortable, country-inspired atmosphere. In contrast, a big, multi-looped bow made of satin ribbon exudes opulence and is suitable for an exquisite, formal setting. By mastering the skill of bow crafting, you may customize your Christmas decorations to represent your personality and the mood you want to create.

Overview of Bow Styles Covered.

This book introduces you to a range of bow styles, each with its particular charm and use. Here's an overview of what you'll learn:

The Simple Single Loop Bow: Beginning with the fundamentals, you'll learn how to make a simple yet lovely bow with a single loop and two tails. It's ideal for adding a delicate accent to little gifts or ornaments.

The Classic Two-Loop Bow: Based on the single loop, this bow has two balanced loops and flowing tails. It's a gift-wrapping must-have that elevates any present.

The Multi-Loop Gift Bow: Enhance your gifts with a bow that has numerous loops, adding depth and dimension. The loops extend out gracefully, giving the bow a luxurious appearance that will certainly impress.

The Floral Pom-Pom Bow: Explore a more elaborate pattern that resembles a budding flower. This bow is made by layering multiple loops in a circular pattern, creating a voluminous, spherical shape ideal for tree toppers or centerpieces.

Wired Ribbon Bows: Discover the versatility of wired ribbons, which maintain their shape and allow you to create stunning bows. These bows are great for huge decorations such as wreaths and garlands.

Layered and Stacked Bows: Discover how to combine multiple ribbons of variable texture, breadth, and color to create multidimensional bows with plenty of detail and visual intrigue.

The Flower-Shaped Bow: Learn how to make bows shaped like flower petals, giving a delicate and beautiful touch to your decor.

The Star Bow: Learn how to fold ribbons into star shapes, which are ideal for adding a cosmic accent to your Christmas decorations.

Each style is supported by clear, thorough instructions that will help you navigate the procedure with ease. We'll also provide you with advice on how to alter these bows, encouraging you to experiment and create your unique designs.

Setting up Your Craft Space

Before you begin your bow-making journey, you must set up a workspace that encourages creativity and efficiency. A well-organized craft space not only enhances the experience but also provides safety and ease.

Choosing Your Workspace

Choose a separate space where you can spread out your materials and work comfortably. This might be a large table in the living area, a kitchen island, or a workstation in a quiet nook. Ensure that the platform is flat and solid, with plenty of room for cutting, folding, and assembling your bow.

Lighting

Good illumination is essential, particularly while working on detailed chores. Position your workspace near a window to benefit from natural light during the day. For evening crafting, choose a bright desk lamp or overhead illumination that lights your work without creating harsh shadows.

Organizing Materials and Tools

Keeping your supplies organized and easily accessible will help you craft more efficiently.

Ribbon Storage: Arrange your ribbons according to color, width, or type. Consider utilizing a ribbon holder or dowel rod—a simple pole that threads through the cores of your ribbon spools, allowing you to pull and cut to the correct length without unraveling the entire spool. Alternatively, translucent plastic boxes or drawers can keep ribbons dust-free while remaining visible.

Tool Kit: Put your essential tools in a container or caddy. This could contain sharp scissors for smooth cuts, wire cutters for trimming floral wire, a glue gun for tight adherence, and measuring tapes or rulers for exact lengths.

Accessories Storage: Sort other things like floral wire, twist ties, and embellishments (such as beads, bells, or imitation greenery) into little boxes or compartments.

Safety considerations

Glue Gun Safety: When not in use, place a heat-resistant mat or silicone pad underneath your hot glue gun. Keep it away from the boundaries of your workplace to avoid unintentional knocks.

Child and Pet Safety: If you have young children or pets, keep sharp tools and small items out of reach when not in use. Be cautious of loose ribbons and cables, which could provide a tripping hazard.

Comfort and Ergonomics

Seating: Select a comfortable chair that promotes proper posture. Crafting sessions can be lengthy, so suitable support can help you stay comfortable.

Work Surface Height: Make sure your table or desk is at a height where you can work without hunching over or straining your shoulders.

Inspirational Atmosphere

Personal touches: Decorate your workstation with items that motivate you, such as a vase of fresh poinsettias, a fragrant candle with hints of pine or cinnamon, or images from previous holiday gatherings.

Play your favorite Christmas music softly in the background to create a festive atmosphere. Melodies can boost your creativity and make the crafting process more fun.

Preparation for cleanup

Place a small trash bin nearby to collect ribbon remnants, wire trims, and other waste materials.

Protective Coverings: If you're worried about glue or marks on your table, lay down a protective cloth or craft mat before you start.

By thoughtfully organizing your craft area, you're setting the stage for a fun and productive bow-making experience. Everything you need will be right at your fingertips, and the welcoming environment will make each session enjoyable.

With your craft room set up and an amazing selection of bow types to choose from, you're well on your way to producing gorgeous, homemade decorations that will brighten your Christmas season. In the next chapters, we'll go over the materials and tools you'll need before beginning our step-by-step journey into the art of bow manufacturing. Let's get started.

Essential Materials and Tools

Beginning your bow-making journey is similar to embarking on a delightful adventure, and as with any voyage, the proper equipment is required. This chapter will walk you through the materials and tools that will become your trusted companions as you create magnificent Christmas bows. You'll learn everything you need to bring your creative thoughts to life, from the luscious textures of various ribbons to the essential tools of the art.

Ribbons and Fabrics

The ribbon is at the center of every beautiful bow, a versatile and expressive medium available in a variety of textures, colors, and finishes. Choosing the proper ribbon is critical since it determines the tone and style of your design.

Types of Ribbons

Satin Ribbon

Consider a smooth, glossy surface that catches the light with a faint sheen, radiating elegance and sophistication.

Satin ribbons are known for their shiny appearance and velvety feel. They drape elegantly, making them perfect for bows with delicate loops and flowing tails. Satin ribbons come in a variety of rich colors and are ideal for formal and luxury designs.

Grosgrain Ribbon

Consider a ribbon with a distinct ribbed texture—strong but flexible, with a matte finish that gives dimension to your bows.

Grosgrain ribbons are resilient and retain their shape well, making them ideal for structured bows. Their texture adds visual interest, and they come in a variety of widths and colors, including brilliant hues and classic neutrals.

Wired Ribbon

Consider a ribbon with thin, nearly undetectable wires woven into the edges, allowing you to shape and sculpt it with ease.

Wired ribbons are quite versatile. The integrated wire adds structure, allowing you to make bows with prominent loops and shapes that retain their shape. They are especially handy for enormous bows used as wreaths, tree toppers, or outdoor decorations.

Velvet Ribbon

Feel the thick, silky nap of velvet beneath your fingertips—a luxuriant texture that brings warmth and richness to any bow.

Velvet ribbons radiate grandeur with their dense pile and rich, vibrant colors. They are ideal for making huge bows, and they look especially good when used in traditional Christmas colors like deep reds and greens.

Burlap Ribbon

Consider the earthy, woven texture of burlap, a rustic fabric that adds a touch of country charm to your projects.

Burlap ribbons are great for rustic or farmhouse-inspired decor. When coupled with more delicate materials such as lace or satin, their natural fibers and neutral tones make for a lovely contrast.

Lace Ribbon

Imagine elaborate patterns of fine threads forming floral motifs and elegant designs, lending a touch of old beauty.

Lace ribbons add a beautiful, feminine touch to your bows. They can be used alone to create a subtle effect, or stacked with other ribbons to enhance texture and depth.

Mesh Ribbon

Consider a lightweight, net-like fabric that gives volume and a fun, airy look to your bows.

Mesh ribbons are ideal for making huge, voluminous bows without adding extra weight. Their open weave lets underlying colors and textures show through, making them ideal for stacking with other ribbons.

Choosing the appropriate ribbon for your project

Choosing the appropriate ribbon requires considering various factors:

Determine the purpose of the bow and where it will be used. For outdoor decorations, choose weather-resistant ribbons such as wired or synthetic fabrics. For gift wrapping, softer ribbons such as satin or grosgrain may be more appropriate.

Desired Aesthetic: Consider the mood you intend to express. Satin or velvet ribbons in rich colors are ideal for a classic and sophisticated design. Bright colors, metallic finishes, or unique textures such as mesh can add a quirky or modern touch.

Color Palette: Think about the existing decor or the wrapping paper you'll be using. To add visual flair, choose complementary or contrasting ribbon colors.

Ribbon Width: Wider ribbons (2.5 inches or more) are good for enormous, statement bows, whereas narrower ribbons (1 inch or less) are best for smaller bows or complex designs.

Texture and Finish: Combine different textures to create depth. Layer a smooth satin with textured burlap or a lace ribbon over a solid hue to create a layered look.

Remember that there are no hard and fast rules; instead, let your creativity guide you. Feel the ribbons in your hands, watch how they drape or keep their shape, and imagine how they will appear in your finished bow.

Tools of Trade

Equipping yourself with the proper tools streamlines the bow-making process while also improving the quality of your work. Here is a list of necessary instruments that will help you craft with precision and simplicity.

Cutting Tools: Scissors

A sharp, dependable pair of scissors is essential. Imagine blades flowing easily through the ribbon, making crisp, clean cuts without fraying the edges.

Invest in scissors designed specifically for ribbons and fabric to keep them sharp. Look for ergonomic handles that are comfortable to use for extended periods.

Rotary Cutters

Consider a portable instrument with a circular blade that glides smoothly over ribbon put on a cutting board, producing straight, accurate lines.

Rotary cutters are ideal for cutting through numerous layers of ribbon or fabric at once. They are very useful when you need to create uniform strips for several bows.

Adhesives Glue Guns

A hot glue gun is required for securing layers of ribbon, attaching embellishments, and fixing ribbon ends to avoid fraying. For complex work, use a glue gun with a fine tip, and to avoid damaging delicate textiles, consider utilizing low-temperature glue sticks.

Fabric Glue

Fabric glue is perfect for applications that require a strong yet undetectable grip. It dries clear and supple, retaining the softness of your ribbons.

Fasteners Floral Wire

Floral wire is ideal for tightening the center of bows, tying bows to wreaths or other decorations, and shaping wired ribbons. Choose green or silver wire, which matches most ribbons.

Twist Ties

fastening and bundling things with a few effortless twists. Twist ties are useful for temporarily holding bows in place before they are securely secured. They are particularly important during the crafting process, as they allow for modifications.

String or cord

Consider a thin, durable string—perhaps in natural jute or cotton—that may be tied snugly around the center of a bow.

String or cable can have both utilitarian and decorative applications. It can be used to secure bows or as a decorative accent when visible.

Measuring Tools:

Rulers

A typical 12-inch ruler is suitable for little tasks, but a longer yardstick may be required for larger bows.

Measuring tape

a flexible tape that can wrap around spools or measure curved edges while maintaining accuracy in all dimensions.

Measuring tapes are vital for measuring longer lengths of ribbon, and they are especially useful when working with huge decorations.

Additional Supplies: Needles and Thread.

A fine needle weaving smoothly through layers of ribbon, connecting them with delicate, practically undetectable stitches.

Certain bows and embellishments may require the use of a needle and thread. Choose a thread that complements your ribbon to keep your stitches hidden.

Pins

Think of skinny pins with tiny heads that keep layers in place without leaving a trace.

Straight pins are useful for holding ribbon layers together while you modify and perfect your bow before final assembly.

Tips for Purchasing Quality Materials on a Budget

Making lovely bows does not have to break the cash. Here are some tips for getting high-quality products at a reasonable price.

Shop sales and clearances.

Keep an eye out for seasonal specials at craft stores, particularly after the holidays, when ribbons and supplies are significantly discounted.

Sign up for emails from your favorite craft stores to get updates on future promotions and unique coupons.

Buy in bulk.

If you intend to make many bows or complete future projects, consider ordering greater quantities of ribbons or supplies.

Bulk purchases frequently result in lower per-unit costs. Sharing a big purchase with friends or other crafters can also be cost-effective.

Explore Discount & Dollar Stores.

Browse the aisles of bargain stores to get ribbons and basic supplies at reduced prices.

While the inventory may vary, some outlets can be treasure troves of low-cost supplies.

Repurpose and recycle.

Look around your home for ribbons from past gifts, clothing, or decorations that can be reused.

Thrift stores and garage sales can also provide unexpected items, such as old ribbons or odd textiles.

Online marketplaces

Search for online platforms where sellers sell materials at competitive prices, frequently with customer reviews to ensure quality.

Websites such as Etsy, eBay, and Amazon may provide discounts, but be aware of shipping fees and delivery timeframes.

Use coupon and loyalty programs.

To save even more money, use craft shop discounts and consider joining their loyalty programs.

Digital coupons and in-store deal alerts are frequently available through these stores' mobile apps.

DIY alternatives

Create your ribbons or embellishments with fabric remnants, paint, or dye.

This not only saves money but also gives your bows a distinct, personal touch.

You lay the groundwork for a successful bow-building project by carefully selecting your materials and providing yourself with the necessary tools. Understanding the properties of various ribbons and having dependable instruments at your disposal will make the creation process easier and more pleasant.

As you assemble your supplies, feel the textures of the ribbons, weigh the scissors in your palm, and become acquainted with your instruments. This tactile connection improves your creative experience, making each bow you make a labor of love.

CHAPTER TWO

Basic Bow-Making Techniques

Starting to make bows is like learning a new language of loops, folds, and knots. This chapter will walk you through the basic techniques for transforming ordinary ribbons into beautiful bows. We'll look at the qualities of various ribbons, learn the fundamentals of folding and looping, how to securely fasten your creations, and the principles of symmetry and proportion. By the end of this chapter, you'll have the skills and confidence to create stunning bows that embody the essence of the Christmas season.

Understanding Ribbon Properties

Before getting into the strategies, it's critical to understand the distinct features of different ribbons. Each type of ribbon acts differently, and recognizing these distinctions will help you select the best ribbon for your chosen bow style.

Flexible and Drape

Satin and Velvet Ribbons: These have a silky, flowing drape. When you hold the length of the satin ribbon by one end, see how it flows smoothly and hangs straight, catching light with its glossy surface. These ribbons are perfect for bows with soft curves and flowing tails.

Grosgrain and burlap ribbons have a ribbed structure and a stronger weave, giving them greater substance. When grasped, they form a little bend instead of hanging straight down. They are ideal for bows with more rigidity and distinct curves.

Wired Ribbons: The inserted wire along the borders allows these ribbons to be shaped while maintaining their shape. You may bend and twist them, and they will maintain the shape you specify, making them ideal for complex and sculpted bows.

Texture and Thickness

Thin Ribbons: Narrow ribbons, less than half an inch wide, are delicate and make tiny bows for small parcels or trinkets.

Thick Ribbons: Wider ribbons, measuring one to three inches or more, create strong statements. They are ideal for huge bows used as focal pieces in your design.

Sheer and lace ribbons offer a touch of elegance and can be used to cover other ribbons. Their transparency lets underlying colors or textures come through, giving your bows more dimension.

Manipulation Behavior Stiffness: Ribbons may be stiffer due to their substance or finish. Stiffer ribbons can hold sharp folds and are less likely to wrinkle, making them ideal for angular bows or those with distinct shapes.

Elasticity: Ribbons with a small elasticity are forgiving when making knots, but they may need extra care to stay in form.

Understanding these characteristics enables you to predict how a ribbon will react when folded, looped, or tied, allowing you to choose the ideal type for your project.

Fundamental Folding and Looping Methods

Folding and looping are fundamental bow-making techniques. Mastering these strategies gives you a solid foundation on which to develop more complicated designs.

The Simple Loop Measuring Ribbon

Cut a length of ribbon to fit your preferred bow size. A little bow can be 12 inches long; larger bows may require several feet.

Creating the first loop:

Hold the ribbon horizontally in front of you. Bring the right end across to the left, producing a teardrop-shaped loop with a downward extending tail.

Adjusting Loop Size:

Slide the loop between your fingers to change its size. Make sure the loop is smooth and there are no twists in the ribbon.

The Classic Two-Loop Bow

It involves creating two loops:

Fold the ribbon back toward the center while holding it horizontally to form a loop on the left side. Repeat on the right side to create a mirror image.

Crossing the loops:

Cross the right loop over the left loop in the center to form an 'X' shape.

Creating the knot:

Bring the right loop beneath the left, then through the center opening. Pull both loops gently to tighten the knot in the center, correcting for symmetry.

The multiple-loop bow with Layering Loops

Start by holding the ribbon tail between your thumb and forefinger. Make a loop to the left, then fold the ribbon back to create a loop to the right. Continue to alternate sides, stacking loops on top of each other.

Maintaining tension:

To prevent the loops from unraveling, keep a firm grasp on the middle where they meet.

Securing the center:

Once you've made the proper number of loops, use floral wire or string to tightly tie the center, securing all loops.

Using Twists for Texture

Adding twists to the ribbon as you make loops can give texture and visual interest. Twist the ribbon in the middle before constructing each new loop, resulting in a spiral effect in the finished bow.

Creating Tails

Symmetric tails:

After you've formed your loops, leave equal lengths of ribbon on each side for tails. Cut the ends at an angle or in a 'V' shape (dovetail) for a polished appearance.

Adjusting Tail Lengths:

For a dramatic appearance, leave longer tails that fall. Trim the tails shorter to create a tidy, compact bow.

Securing bows with knots, wires, and adhesives

Properly securing your bow guarantees that it keeps its shape and lasts the entire holiday season.

Using Knots Center Knot:

For smaller bows, a tight knot in the center may suffice. Make sure the knot is snug to keep the loops from loosening.

Double knots:

Tie a second knot for increased security. Be careful not to overtighten, since this can cause the ribbon to pucker.

Cut the floral wire.

Using wire cutters, cut a piece of floral wire about six inches long.

Wrapping the center:

Wrap the wire around the bow from front to back, crossing the ends.

Twist to Secure:

Twist the wire ends tightly around the back of the bow. The wire should compress the ribbon tightly without cutting through it.

Concealing the wire:

Wrap a little piece of ribbon around the middle of the wire and secure it with glue.

Adhesives: Hot Glue.

To fix the ribbon ends or attach embellishments, apply a small dab of hot glue. Avoid using too much adhesive, as it can seep out and become visible.

Fabric Glue:

Fabric adhesive provides a more flexible bond, particularly when working with delicate ribbons.

Twist Ties and String for Temporary Holds.

Twist ties are useful for securing the bow while you tweak the loops and tails. They can be removed once the bow is securely fastened.

String Ties:

A thin rope or cable can be wound securely around the center. Choose a color that matches the ribbon or will be covered later.

Mastering Symmetry and Proportion

A well-crafted bow is visually appealing, with balanced loops and tails. Achieving symmetry and proportion is an art that requires experience.

Balancing Loops: Even Loops

As you make loops on either side, make sure they are similar in size. Hold the bow up and visually compare the loops, making any necessary adjustments.

Layering loops:

When producing multi-loop bows, each consecutive loop might be somewhat smaller than the preceding one to get a layered look.

Proportional tail length:

The tails should match the size of the loops. Longer tails lend grace to larger bows, while shorter tails keep the design unified on smaller bows.

Angle and shape:

Cut tails at matching angles or in complementary forms to improve symmetry.

Center Alignment: Central Knot or Wrap.

Ensure that the knot or center wrap is directly in the center of the bow. This focal point serves to anchor the design.

Consistent tightness:

The tightness of your securing method should be uniform so that one side does not appear fuller than the other.

Practice Exercises to Improve Your Skills

To gain confidence and improve your technique, try these exercises:

Exercise 1: Single Loop Precision Goal:

Make numerous single-loop bows with the same loop sizes and tail lengths.

Method:

Use a measuring tape to cut ribbon lengths exactly. Practice making the loop and securing the center, with an emphasis on consistency.

Exercise 2: Multi-Loop Variation Objective:

Create a multi-loop bow and play with varying numbers of loops.

Method:

Begin with four loops (two on each side), then progress to six or eight, watching how the bow's fullness changes.

Exercise 3: Symmetry Challenge - Goal:

Make an asymmetrical bow and then tweak it to reach perfect symmetry.

Method:

Make different-sized loops, then practice manipulating them to balance the bow by gently pulling on the loops and tails.

Exercise 4 - Texture Mixing Goal:

Create a single bow with ribbons of varying textures and widths.

Method:

Layer a sheer ribbon over a solid one, or combine a satin ribbon and a grosgrain. Examine how the various materials interact.

Exercise 5 - Securing Techniques Goal:

Try out several methods of securing bows and evaluate their efficiency.

Method:

Make identical bows and bind one with a knot, one with floral wire, and another with glue. Determine which method offers the best hold and appearance for each bow type.

By doing these activities, you'll gain a keen eye for detail and a deft touch with your materials. Remember that practice is essential—don't be disheartened by early mistakes. Each bow you manufacture moves you closer to mastering the craft.

CHAPTER THREE

Simple Single Loop Bow

The basic single-loop bow is a timeless classic, charming in its simplicity but adaptable in its application. It's an excellent starting point for new crafters and a must-have for expert ones. In this chapter, we'll walk you through the process of making this charming bow, look at several sizes and ribbon types, and talk about how you may use it in your Christmas decor.

Step-by-step instructions

Materials needed:

Ribbon of your choice (at least 12" long)

Scissors

Optional: Floral Wire or String

Optional: Glue gun, fabric glue

Instructions:

Prepare your ribbon.

Lay the ribbon flat on a clean, smooth surface.

Measure and cut a ribbon length that is acceptable for your bow. A little bow can be 12 inches long; a larger bow may require 24 inches or more.

Create a loop:

Hold one end of the ribbon in your left hand and let the rest extend to the right.

Form a loop by bringing the ribbon's right end over to the left. The ribbon should extend about an inch beyond the point where you hold it with your left hand.

Change the size of the loop to your liking. The larger the loop, the bigger the bow will be.

Form the bow's center:

Pinch the ribbon where the ends overlap. This pressure point will be your bow's core.

Make sure the loop is flat and that the ribbon is not twisted.

Secure the center.

Option 1: Knot Method.

If your ribbon is narrow and flexible, you can make a basic knot.

Wrap the tail end of the ribbon around the pinch point.

Tie a tight knot at the rear of the bow to hold the loop in place.

Option 2: Wire/String Method

Place a little piece of floral wire or string over the front center of the bow, where you pinched it.

Wrap the wire around to the back and twist tightly to form the loop.

Trim any excess wire and tuck it securely behind the bow.

Option 3: Glue Method.

Apply a little amount of hot glue or fabric adhesive to the pinch point.

Press hard and hold for a few seconds until the glue has cured.

Adjust and shape the bow:

Pull gently on the loop to alter its size and ensure it is symmetrical.

Smooth any wrinkles or twists in the ribbon.

Create Tails (Optional):

The tails will be made of any surplus ribbon that extends from the knot or wire.

Adjust the tails to be identical in length on both sides.

Use scissors to neatly clip the ends. You can cut them straight across, diagonally, or make a 'V' form dovetail by folding the ribbon in half lengthwise and cutting at an angle from the folded edge out.

Ribbon Variations

Ribbon size variation

Miniature bows:

Use a narrow ribbon (1/4-1/2 inch wide).

Ideal for decorating tiny gift boxes, ornaments, and place settings.

To make petite loops, cut the ribbon into shorter lengths (6 to 8 inches).

Large bows:

Use a wide ribbon (2 inches or more).

Ideal for adorning larger gifts, wreaths, and Christmas trees.

To create generous loops, cut longer ribbon (24 inches or more).

Ribbon Type Variations:

Satin Ribbons:

Provides a smooth, lustrous appearance.

Creates lovely bows suited for formal settings.

Grosgrain ribbon:

Creates a rough, ribbed surface.

Adds a bit of informal charm to rustic or whimsical themes.

Velvet Ribbon:

Provides a luxuriant, plush appearance.

Ideal for producing rich, sumptuous bows.

Burlap or jute ribbon:

Provides a rustic, natural feel.

Complements country or farmhouse-style decor.

Sheer or organza ribbon:

Provides a delicate, airy appearance.

Adds a subtle touch to decorations without overpowering them.

Layering ribbons:

Combine two ribbons with varying widths and textures.

Before you make the loop, layer a smaller ribbon on top of a wider one.

This provides depth and interest to your bow.

Applications for Single Loop Bows in Decor

The simple single-loop bow may be modest, but there are numerous applications:

Gift Wrapping:

For a classic touch, attach the bow to the top of a wrapped present.

Use ribbon colors that suit your wrapping paper.

Christmas Tree Decorations:

Hang the bows directly on the tree branches.

Use bows as ornament embellishments by attaching them to bauble hooks.

Wreath Embellishments:

Add color and texture to a wreath by placing bows equally around it.

Place bows at the base of floral arrangements within the wreath.

Table Settings:

Tie bows around napkins to create a beautiful place setting.

Tie bows to the stems of wine glasses or the backs of chairs.

Home Decor Accents:

Decorate doorknobs, cabinet handles, and staircase banisters with bows.

Attach ribbons to candle holders or vases to add a festive touch.

Gift Bags and Tags:

Attach ribbons to the present bag handles.

Use little bows on gift tags to add appeal.

Remember that the simplicity of the single-loop bow allows it to fit smoothly into a variety of decor styles, making it an essential component of your holiday decorating repertoire.

CHAPTER FOUR

The Classic Two-Loop Bow

Building on the single-loop bow, the classic two-loop bow adds symmetry and fullness, resulting in a more traditional and identifiable bow design. This technique is adaptable and gives a sophisticated touch to presents and decorations. In this chapter, we'll look at how to make balanced loops, how to get tight centers, and innovative methods to employ two-loop bows in Christmas gift wrapping.

Creating Balanced Loops

Materials needed:

Ribbon (about 18 to 24 inches for a medium-sized bow)

Scissors

Floral Wire or String

Optional: Glue gun or fabric glue.

Instructions:

Prepare your ribbon.

Cut a length of ribbon appropriate for the size of the bow you want to construct.

Create the first loop.

Hold the ribbon horizontally with both hands, the left end between your thumb and index finger on the left, and the right end in your right hand.

Bring the left end of the ribbon to the middle, creating a loop that points to the right. The tail should extend down from the middle.

Create the second loop.

Bring the right end of the ribbon into the center, crossing over the first loop to create a second loop that points to the left. This loop should be identical to the first one.

Adjust each loop to be of similar size. The ribbon should now look like a figure eight or an infinity sign.

Pinch the center:

Pinch the middle where the loops and tails meet with your thumb and forefinger.

Ensure that the loops are symmetrical, modifying as needed.

Secure the center.

Using Floral Wire:

Place a piece of floral wire in front of the pinched center.

Wrap it securely around the back and twist it to fasten.

Trim any excess wire and tuck it behind the bow.

Using Strings:

Tie a length of string or thin cord tightly around the center and knot it securely at the back.

Adjust the bow:

Gently pull and shape the loops to ensure they are equal and rounded.

Arrange the tails so that they hang down properly.

Finish the tails:

Trim the tails to the desired length.

Cut the ends in a similar style—straight across, angled, or dovetail finish.

Techniques for Tight Centers

A tight center is essential for a professional appearance and helps the bow retain its shape.

Tips:

Firm pinch:

When gathering the center, use strong pressure to keep the ribbon compressed.

Secure wrapping:

Wrap floral wire or thread tightly around the pinched center many times, if needed.

The tighter the wrap, the more pronounced the central knot will be.

Center Knot Embellishment:

Cover the middle with a thin piece of ribbon to create a seamless look.

Cut a short ribbon (approximately 2 inches).

Place it in the front middle of the bow.

Wrap it around to the back and overlap the ends.

Secure the ends with a small amount of hot glue or fabric adhesive.

Avoid bulky centers.

When securing the core, keep the mass to a minimum.

Thin wire or string is preferred over thick cords or numerous layers of ribbon.

Practice for Perfection:

Consistent pressure:

Maintain continuous pressure while pinching and securing the center.

This holds the loops tightly without crushing them.

Adjusting after Securing:

After fastening the center, spend some time adjusting the loops and tails.

Fluff the loops by gradually expanding and curling them outwards.

Decorating Gift Packages

The classic two-loop bow is a popular choice for gift wrapping, giving a touch of refinement to your items.

Ideas for gift wrapping:

Centrepiece Bow:

Place the bow in the center of the gift, atop the crisscrossed ribbons that wrap around it.

Use a small bit of adhesive or tie the bow directly on the wrapped ribbons.

Asymmetrical Placement:

To add a modern twist, position the bow off-center or in a corner.

This pairs well with minimalist wrapping paper designs.

Layered ribbons:

Use a contrasting ribbon to make the bow stand out against the wrapping paper or underlying ribbon.

For example, a gold satin bow on deep red paper makes a joyful contrast.

Embellishments:

To add ornamentation, place little baubles, bells, or sprigs of holly beneath the bow.

Before tying the bow, incorporate these parts into the center to secure them.

Coordinating with the wrapping paper:

Color Harmony:

Choose ribbon colors that match or contrast with your wrapping paper.

Monochromatic schemes (various shades of the same color) can look classy.

Texture Play:

Create visual interest by pairing glossy ribbons with matte paper, or vice versa.

Use textured ribbons such as grosgrain or velvet to enhance depth.

Special touches:

Personalized Tags:

Attach a gift tag beneath the bow with a matching ribbon or string.

Handwrite the recipient's name to add a personal touch.

Reusability:

Encourage sustainability by creating bows that can be removed and reused.

Secure the bow with a removable adhesive or tie it so it can be easily taken off.

By mastering the classic two-loop bow, you've gained a practical and elegant weapon for your crafting arsenal. Whether embellishing gifts, improving decorations, or simply enjoying the art of bow-making, this style provides limitless opportunities for creativity and personal expression.

CHAPTER FIVE

The Multi-Loop Gift Bow

The multi-loop gift bow is a great way to add elegance and flair to your gifts. Its abundance of loops and layers adds luxury to every gift-giving event. In this chapter, we'll look at how to construct volume, layer for depth, and customize your bows with various ribbon widths to achieve amazing, professional-looking results.

Increasing Volume with Multiple Loops

Materials needed:

Ribbon of your choosing (at least 3 yards for a medium-sized bow)

Scissors

Floral Wire or String

Optional: Glue gun or fabric glue.

Instructions:

Prepare your ribbon.

Choose a flexible yet durable ribbon, such as satin or wired ribbon.

Ribbons should be measured and cut to the desired length. A complete bow requires roughly 3 yards (9 feet).

Creating Loops:

Start with the tail (optional):

Leave a length of ribbon (about 12 inches) hanging down to act as one of the tails.

Pinch the ribbon where you want the bow to start.

Form the first loop:

Bring the ribbon from the pinch point up and back toward yourself to form a loop on the left side.

The amount of this loop determines the total size of your bow.

Pinch and twist:

Pinch the ribbon near the base of the loop.

Twist the ribbon half a turn so that the correct side (front) faces outward.

Form the second loop:

Bring the ribbon to the right side, forming a loop that mimics the first.

Pinch and twist again at the central place.

Continue adding loops:

Alternate sides to form loops of equal size.

After each loop, pinch and twist in the center.

For a medium-sized bow, strive for 4 to 6 loops on each side (a total of 8 to 12 loops).

Maintaining Even Loop Size:

Visual checks:

After each set of loops, stop to ensure that they are symmetric.

Before attaching, carefully tug on the loops to adjust their size.

Securing the center:

Using Floral Wire:

Place a piece of floral wire over the front center of the bow, where you are pinching the loops.

Wrap it securely around the back and firmly twist it to secure all of the layers.

Ensure that the wire is tight enough to hold the loops in place without cutting the ribbon.

Creating Tails:

Second Tail:

After attaching the center, leave a length of ribbon equal to the first tail.

Cut the ribbon cleanly.

Shaping the bow:

Fluff the Loops:

Separate the loops by gently tugging them outward from the center.

Arrange them so that they fan out evenly, resulting in a full, rounded appearance.

Adjusting for volume:

To maintain the fullness of wired ribbons, bend and shape the loops.

To keep non-wired ribbons from flattening, carefully adjust the loops.

Finishing the tails:

Styling the ends:

Trim the tails to the desired length.

Cut the ends in a 'V' shape (dovetail) or at an angle for a polished appearance.

Layering Techniques For Depth

Adding layers to your bow adds depth and visual intrigue, helping it stand out even more.

Method 1: Layering Ribbons with the Same Width

Double looping:

Continue looping to create numerous levels of loops.

Make eight loops on each side instead of four.

This increases the bow's density and fullness.

Offsetting Loops:

After establishing the initial set of loops, make other loops that are somewhat smaller in size.

Place these on top of the original set, offsetting them to fill up any gaps.

Method 2: Combining various ribbon widths

Base Layer:

For the bottom layer of loops, use a wider ribbon (2.5 inches or more).

Top Layers:

Use a smaller ribbon (1 to 1.5 inches wide) in a similar color or texture.

Make more loops and arrange them on top of the basic layer.

Securing Layers Together:

Stack the layers and align the centers.

Use floral wire to secure both layers simultaneously.

Method 3: Combining Textures and Patterns

Alternating ribbons:

Use two separate ribbons of equal width.

Alternate between the two ribbons as you make each loop.

Visual contrast:

Combine a solid-colored ribbon with a patterned one.

The clashing designs provide depth and intrigue.

Customizing using various ribbon widths

Using ribbons of varied widths can transform the look of your bow.

Using wide ribbons:

Impactful Presence:

Wide ribbons (3 inches or more) make enormous, bold bows.

Perfect for large gifts or striking decorations

Ease of shaping

Wide, wired ribbons hold shapes well and make for dramatic loops.

Use Narrow Ribbons:

Delicate details:

Narrow ribbons (less than 1 inch) make smaller loops.

Ideal for adding complex detailing to larger bows or embellishing little items

Layering possibilities:

Use several narrow ribbons together.

Make a multi-loop bow by arranging numerous threads side by side.

Combining widths:

Dynamic Look:

Begin with a base of broader loops.

Add thinner loops on top to increase height and depth.

Color Coordination:

Use a distinct hue for each breadth to improve visual appeal.

Creative ideas:

Add a centerpiece.

Put a decorative accent in the center, such as a jeweled brooch, a little decoration, or a silk flower.

Secure it over the knot or wire.

Incorporate Tails into Loops:

Instead of leaving the tails hanging, incorporate them into other loops.

This results in a fuller bow with no excess ribbon.

Applications:

Gift boxes:

For a stunning display, use the multi-loop bow on top of large gift boxes.

To get a unified effect, match the ribbon colors to the wrapping paper.

Decorations:

Use these bows as tree toppers or to decorate garlands and mantels.

Attach them to wreaths for extra volume and color.

Mastering the multi-loop gift bow allows you to create opulent, eye-catching decorations that elevate any gift or situation. Experiment with different ribbons, layers, and techniques to find your style.

CHAPTER SIX

The Floral Pom-pom Bow

The floral pom-pom bow is a lovely explosion of loops that looks like a budding flower or a celebratory pom-pom. It's ideal for bringing a quirky touch to wreaths, centerpieces, and larger decorations. In this chapter, we'll learn how to make full, round bows, combine colors and textures, and use them to decorate your home for the holidays.

Materials required for crafting full, round shapes include:

Ribbon (fabric or paper ribbon works well; approximately 4 to 6 yards)

Scissors

Floral wire

Optional: Stapler for paper ribbon

Instructions:

Choose your ribbon:

Choose a lightweight ribbon that is easy to manage.

Wired ribbon is optional, but it can assist keep the shape.

Preparing the ribbon:

Continuous Loop Method:

Cut a ribbon about 4 to 6 yards long.

Use more ribbon to create a bigger bow.

Creating the accordion fold:

Fold the ribbon:

Begin at one end of the ribbon.

Fold the ribbon back and forth in an accordion (zig-zag) pattern, with each fold about 4 to 6 inches long.

Fold the ribbon until it forms a stack.

Securing the center:

Find the middle:

To determine the middle point, fold the layered ribbon in half.

You can delicately mark this point with a pencil or crease it.

Notch the sides (optional for thicker ribbons)

Cut small notches on both sides of the stack toward the middle.

Take care not to cut too deeply; the notches should be about one-third the width of the ribbon.

This allows the ribbon to spread out more easily.

Attach the floral wire.

Wrap a length of floral wire securely around the center of the stack.

Twist the wire securely in the back.

Shaping the bow:

Separate the layers.

Gently spread the folds on either side of the center.

Lift the top layer of ribbon from one side and fluff it out as you pull it towards the center.

Continue layering:

Repeat with each succeeding layer, tugging and fluffing as you go.

Maintain symmetry by alternating sides.

Forming the round shape:

As you pull and arrange the layers, a full, spherical pom-pom will form.

Adjust the loops to cover any gaps and get an equal, spherical shape.

Finishing touches:

Trim the edges (optional).

Before folding the ribbon, round the edges to give it a softer appearance.

Alternatively, trim the edges into points for a more dynamic look.

Color and texture combinations

of multi-colored pom-poms

Layering Different Colors:

Before folding, stack ribbons of different colors.

When fluffed, the hues blend, giving a vivid, multicolored look.

Alternating Colors:

Alternate ribbons of various colors or patterns in the accordion folds.

When the bow is fluffed, it gives the appearance of being striped or patterned.

Mixing Textures:

Combine Various Ribbon Types:

Layer translucent organza ribbon between solid satin or grosgrain ribbons.

The sheer ribbon is transparent, which gives depth and dimension.

Incorporate Decorative Elements.

To add dazzle, use lace, tulle, or even thin strands of metallic ribbon.

To give texture, mix in pieces of fabric or lightweight mesh.

Decoration ideas for wreaths and centerpieces include

Centrepiece Bow:

Place the floral pom-pom bow at the bottom center or top of a wreath.

Secure it with the floral wire used to knot the bow and wrap it around the wreath frame.

Complementary elements:

Decorate the bow with holly sprigs, pinecones, or ornaments.

Select ribbon colors that compliment the wreath's vegetation.

Table centerpieces:

Standalone Decorations:

Use the bow as a solitary centerpiece for your dining table.

Place it on a beautiful plate or charger to give a touch of sophistication.

Combined with candles:

Place the bow around the base of a pillar candle or candelabra.

Keep the ribbon at a safe distance from any open flames.

Garlands & Swags:

Intermittent accents:

Attach smaller pom-pom bows to garlands draped over mantels or staircases.

To get a cohesive appearance, space them equally.

Tree Decorations:

Unique ornaments:

Hang small pom-pom bows as Christmas tree ornaments.

Use a range of colors and textures to generate interest.

Tree Topper:

Make a larger pom-pom bow to decorate the top of your tree.

Unlike standard star or angel toppers, it offers a gentle, whimsical touch.

Creative Tips:

Adding scent:

Spray the bow lightly with a holiday-scented room spray (such as pine or cinnamon) to add aroma to your decor.

Test on a small area first to check that it does not stain the ribbon.

Embellishments:

Add little trinkets, jingle bells, or imitation berries to the middle of the bow.

Use hot glue or bind them together with floral wire.

Variations:

Using paper ribbon:

To make a pom-pom bow, use paper ribbon or gift wrap.

This is inexpensive and allows for a diverse selection of colors and designs.

When using paper, staple the center instead of using wire.

Creating a Tiered Pom-pom:

Create two pom-pom bows of varying sizes.

Stack the smaller one on top of the larger, locking them together in the middle.

This increases height and fullness.

Practical applications:

Gift Packaging:

Attach a pom-pom bow to the top of a gift for a festive and colorful display.

Choose colors that match or enhance the wrapping paper.

Party decorations:

Use pom-pom bows to decorate holiday events.

They can be hung from the ceiling or placed throughout the area to create a joyful mood.

Photo backdrops:

Make a collection of pom-pom bows in different sizes and colors.

Arrange them on a wall to create a decorative backdrop for Christmas photos.

By mastering the flowery pom-pom bow, you've added a fun and festive touch to your bow-making abilities. This adaptable pattern adds fun and whimsy to any situation, making your Christmas decorations truly special.

In these chapters, we've looked at advanced bow-making techniques that will broaden your creative horizons. The multi-loop gift bow and flowery pom-pom bow allow you to play with volume, layering, and texture. As you practice and improve your talents, you'll discover countless ways to use handcrafted bows to enhance your Christmas decor.

Remember that patience and imagination are essential components of successful bow crafting. Don't be scared to experiment with different combinations and personalize each bow. Happy creating!

CHAPTER SEVEN

Wired Ribbon Bows

Wired ribbon bows have revolutionized the bow-making industry. The concealed wires along the ribbon's edges provide flexibility and structure, allowing you to make bows with shapes and dimensions that would be difficult to achieve with a normal ribbon. In this chapter, we'll look at the benefits of utilizing wired ribbons, learn about shaping and sculpting techniques, and walk you through the process of making dynamic tree toppers that will be the highlight of your holiday decor.

Advantages of Using Wired Ribbons: - Structural Integrity

Shape Retention: The ribbon's edges are studded with wire, allowing the bow to easily keep its shape. Once molded, the loops and tails remain in place, ensuring a polished appearance throughout the Christmas season.

Durability: Wired ribbons are stronger than non-wired ribbons, making them perfect for decorations that must tolerate handling or outdoor environments.

Design Versatility

Three-Dimensional Effects: Using wired ribbons, you may make bows with volume and depth, loops that stand straight, and tails that curl elegantly.

Sculpting Possibilities: The wire allows you to twist, curl, or fan out the ribbon, expanding your creative possibilities beyond standard bow shapes.

Easy to use

User-Friendly: The wire's stiffness makes manipulating the ribbon easier, particularly for novices. The ribbon keeps the folds and curves as you stitch, which eliminates the aggravation of floppy loops.

Variety of options

A wide selection: Wired ribbons are available in a wide range of materials, colors, and patterns, including metallics and glittering finishes, sheer organza, and rustic burlap, giving you plenty of options to suit any decorating motif.

Shaping and Sculpting Techniques

Mastering the skill of manipulating wired ribbons allows you to make bows that are both expressive and visually appealing.

Basic Shaping

Forming Strong Loops

Technique: After making the loops for your bow, gently spread them apart. Use your fingers to open each loop, giving it a rounded, complete shape.

Tip: For a more dramatic look, make the loops larger and fluff them outward to form a large bow.

Curling tails

To curl the tails, run the ribbon between your thumb and the blade of a pair of scissors (similar to how you would curl a balloon ribbon). The wire will help the tail keep its curl.

Alternative: Wrap the tail around a cylindrical item, such as a dowel or marker, then slide it off to create a spiral curl.

Advanced sculpting

Creating Spirals and Twists

Spirals: Tightly twist the ribbon from one end to the other. The wire will support the spiral curve, providing a dynamic aspect to your bow.

Twists: After you've formed your bow, twist individual loops to face different ways to provide movement and depth.

Forming Waves and Ruffles

To achieve a wavy or ruffled effect, gently bend the ribbon back and forth along the wired edge. This creates texture and visual intrigue.

Shape into Figures

Bend and curve the wired ribbon to form shapes such as hearts, stars, or flowers. This is perfect for constructing theme-based decorations.

Secure Your Shapes

Floral Wire Reinforcement: If necessary, apply more floral wire to secure intricate shapes. Wrap the wire discretely around any spots that require additional support.

Hot glue can be used to secure folds or intersections in permanent arrangements, guaranteeing that your design remains intact.

Creating dynamic tree toppers

A magnificent tree topper adds the finishing touch to your Christmas tree, while a wired ribbon bow may make a dramatic and elegant statement.

Materials needed

Wide wired ribbon (at least 2.5 to 4 inches wide by 3 to 5 yards long)

Scissors

Floral wire

Optional: Decorative picks (such as imitation sprigs, decorations, and feathers)

Instructions

Prepare your ribbon.

Choose a ribbon that goes well with the colors on your tree.

Make sure you have enough length to make a large bow with several loops.

Create the bow.

Form large loops.

Begin by dangling a tail of ribbon (approximately 18 inches) down.

Create a loop by bringing the ribbon up and back to the middle, twisting it at the base to keep the right side facing out.

Continue to make loops, switching sides and twisting in the center after each loop.

For a full bow, add at least 5 to 6 loops on each side.

Secure the center.

Wrap the floral wire tightly around the center of the bow.

Leave enough wire to attach the bow to the tree.

Add Decorative Elements (Optional).

Incorporate Picks.

Place colorful picks or sprigs between the loops before fixing the center.

This increases height and visual intrigue.

Attach ornaments.

Use hot glue or wire to attach ornaments to the bow's center or edges.

Shape the bow.

Fluff the Loops.

Each loop should be gently pulled and spread to form spherical shapes.

Use the wire's edges to place the loops upward, outward, or in any other orientation.

Style the tails.

Allow the tails to trickle down the tree.

Curl or wave the tails using the shaping techniques we described before.

Attach the bow to the tree.

Positioning

Place the bow at the very top of the tree, keeping it centered and balanced.

Securing

Wrap the ends of the floral wire around the tree trunk or top branch.

Twist the wire tightly to secure the bow in place.

Final adjustments

Step back and look at the tree topper from various perspectives.

Adjust the loops and tails to ensure symmetry and fullness.

Creative Variations

Multiple ribbons

Use two or more ribbons with various designs or textures to create depth.

Layer a sheer ribbon over a solid one to create a brilliant appearance.

Illumination

To create a dazzling centerpiece, weave battery-operated LED lights into the bow.

Safety considerations

Ensure that any electrical components are safe and do not produce heat that could damage the ribbon.

By utilizing the adaptability of wired ribbons, you may design bows that are both visually appealing and structurally outstanding. Wired ribbon bows, whether used to decorate your tree, enhance wreaths, or garnish gifts, provide a professional and elegant touch to your holiday decorations.

CHAPTER EIGHT

Layered and Stacked Bows

Layered and stacked bows are all about complexity and extravagance. By combining different ribbons, patterns, and embellishments, you can create bows that are rich in detail and make a bold statement. In this chapter, we'll explore how to mix ribbon types and patterns, assemble multi-tiered designs, and add embellishments that elevate your bows to the next level.

Mixing Ribbon Types and Patterns

Choosing Complementary Ribbons

Color Harmony: Select ribbons that share a common color palette or theme to ensure cohesion.

Texture Contrast: Pair smooth ribbons like satin with textured ones like burlap or grosgrain to create tactile interest.

Pattern Mixing: Combine patterns thoughtfully—stripes with polka dots, or solids with florals—ensuring one pattern doesn't overpower the other.

Layering Techniques

Direct Layering

Base Ribbon: Start with the widest ribbon as your base.

Top Ribbon: Place a narrower ribbon on top of the base ribbon, aligning the centers.

Securing Together: Treat the two ribbons as a single piece when forming loops.

Alternating Ribbons

Loop Variation: Alternate ribbons for each loop. For example, the first loop is made with one ribbon, and the next with another.

Visual Effect: This creates a striped appearance in the finished bow.

Offset Layering

Slight Offset: Layer ribbons slightly off-center to reveal the bottom ribbon beneath the top layer.

Dimension: This adds depth and a shadow effect to your bow.

Assembling Multi-Tiered Designs

Creating Multiple Layers

Prepare Ribbons

Cut lengths of different ribbons, varying in width and pattern.

Form Individual Bows

Create separate bows with each type of ribbon, using the techniques from earlier chapters.

Ensure each bow is slightly smaller than the previous one to allow for visible layering.

Stacking the Bows

Place the smallest bow on top of the larger one.

Align the centers or rotate them slightly for a fuller appearance.

Securing the Layers

Use floral wire or string to tie all the bows together tightly at the center.

Wrap the wire securely and conceal it with a small piece of ribbon or an embellishment.

Shaping the Stacked Bow

Fluffing Loops

Gently separate and arrange the loops of each layer.

Spread them out to create an even, rounded shape.

Adjusting Tails

Allow tails from each layer to hang freely.

Trim them at varying lengths for a cascading effect.

Adding Embellishments for Extra Flair

Types of Embellishments

Artificial Greenery

Sprigs of Pine or Holly: Tuck small pieces between loops for a festive touch.

Ornaments and Baubles

Miniature Decorations: Attach small ornaments, bells, or snowflakes to the center or edges of the bow.

Beads and Jewels

Sparkle and Shine: Glue rhinestones or pearls onto the ribbon surfaces.

Feathers and Tulle

Texture and Movement: Incorporate feathers or pieces of tulle for a whimsical effect.

Attachment Techniques

Hot Glue

Quick and Secure: Use a hot glue gun to attach embellishments firmly.

Wiring

Floral Picks: Many decorative items come on stems that can be wired into the bow's center.

Sewing

Discreet and Durable: Use needle and thread to stitch embellishments onto the ribbon.

Design Considerations

Balance

Symmetry: Distribute embellishments evenly to maintain balance.

Theme Cohesion

Consistent Style: Choose embellishments that match the overall theme of your decor, whether it's rustic, elegant, or whimsical.

Avoid Overcrowding

Less is More: Be selective to prevent the bow from appearing cluttered.

Applications

Gift Enhancements

Use layered and embellished bows to make presents stand out under the tree.

Home Decor

Adorn mantels, staircases, or entryways with these ornate bows to create focal points.

Event Decorations

Perfect for holiday parties or weddings, these bows can elevate the ambiance of any event space.

By mastering layered and stacked bows, you've added an artistic and luxurious dimension to your bow-making skills. The combination of different ribbons and embellishments allows you to express your creativity fully, resulting in unique and eye-catching decorations.

CHAPTER NINE

The Flower-Shaped Bow

The flower-shaped bow brings the elegance and beauty of blossoms into your holiday decor. Resembling petals and blooms, these bows are not only perfect for Christmas but can be adapted for any occasion year-round. In this chapter, we'll guide you through crafting petal and bloom structures, integrating fabric and ribbon, and exploring decorative uses beyond the holidays.

Crafting Petal and Bloom Structures

Materials Needed

Ribbon or fabric strips (various lengths and widths)

Scissors

Needle and thread or hot glue

Button or decorative gem for the center (optional)

Instructions

Prepare Your Petals

Cut Strips

Cut multiple strips of ribbon or fabric, each of the same length. The length will determine the size of your petals; for a medium flower, 6-inch strips work well.

Number of Petals

Prepare 6 to 8 strips for a full flower. More strips result in a fuller bloom.

Forming the Petals

Looping

Take one strip and bring the two ends together, forming a loop with the right side of the ribbon facing out.

Ensure the ends overlap slightly.

Securing

Use a small dot of hot glue or a stitch to secure the ends together.

Repeat this process for all strips.

Assembling the Flower

Creating the Base Layer

Arrange four loops in a circle, with the joined ends meeting at the center.

Securing

Stitch or glue the centers together where the ends meet.

Adding Layers

Place additional loops on top of the base layer, offsetting them to fill the gaps between petals.

Secure each layer as you go.

Finishing the Center

Centerpiece

Attach a button, bead, or decorative gem to the center to conceal the joined ends and add a focal point.

Alternative

Create a smaller loop or rolled rosette from the ribbon to serve as the flower's center.

Adjusting the Petals

Shaping

Gently pull and spread the petals to create fullness.

For wired ribbons, you can bend the edges to mimic the curvature of natural petals.

Using Fabric and Ribbon Together

Combining Materials

Fabric Petals

Use fabric such as satin, organza, or tulle to create softer, more delicate petals.

Layering

Alternate layers of ribbon and fabric for a textured look.

Frayed Edges

For a rustic or shabby-chic effect, use fabrics that fray slightly at the edges, adding character to your flower.

Techniques

Singeing Edges

Carefully run the edges of synthetic fabric petals near a flame to prevent fraying and give a curled effect.

Gathering

Create ruffled petals by sewing a running stitch along one edge of a fabric strip and pulling the thread to gather it.

CHAPTER TEN

The Star Bow

The star bow is a radiant and festive design that captures the magic of the holiday season. With its crisp lines and shimmering surfaces, it's an eye-catching addition to gifts and decorations. In this chapter, we'll explore folding techniques to create star shapes, incorporating metallic and glitter ribbons, and tips for perfecting the star bow for gift wrapping.

Folding Techniques for Star Shapes

Materials Needed

Ribbon (preferably wired, 1 to 2 inches wide)

Scissors

Stapler or hot glue

Optional: Decorative center embellishment

Instructions

Prepare Your Ribbon

Cut two lengths of ribbon, each about 12 inches long.

Forming the Loops

First Loop

Take one ribbon piece and form a loop by bringing one end to the other, overlapping slightly.

Flatten the loop, creating a figure that resembles an awareness ribbon.

Creating a Twist

Twist the loop at the center so that both ends are now pointing downward, forming a shape similar to an eight-pointed star.

Securing the Center

Staple Method

Staple the center where the ribbons cross to hold the shape.

Glue Method

Apply a small dot of hot glue at the intersection to secure it.

Repeat with the Second Ribbon

Create an identical loop and secure it in the same way.

Assembling the Star

Layering

Place one looped ribbon on top of the other, offsetting them so the points of the star are evenly spaced.

Securing Together

Staple or glue the centers together.

Finishing Touches

Center Embellishment

Add a decorative button, gem, or small ornament to the center to conceal any staples or glue.

Adjusting the Points

Spread out the loops to ensure the star shape is symmetrical.

Incorporating Metallic and Glitter Ribbons

Choosing the Right Ribbon

Metallic Ribbons

Reflective Shine: Gold, silver, or copper ribbons add a luxurious sheen.

Festive Appeal: Metallics are synonymous with holiday glamour.

Glitter Ribbons

Sparkle and Dazzle: Glittered ribbons catch the light, adding a dynamic sparkle to your bows.

Texture: The rough texture of glitter adds visual interest.

Tips for Working with Glitter Ribbons

Sealing Edges

Use clear nail polish or fabric sealant on cut edges to prevent fraying and shedding.

Minimizing Mess

Work over a sheet of paper or tray to catch excess glitter.

Perfecting the Star for Gift Wrapping

Attachment Methods

Double-Sided Tape

Apply tape to the back of the bow for a clean, invisible attachment to the gift.

Glue Dots

Use adhesive dots for a strong hold without the mess of liquid glue.

Placement on Gifts

Center Position

Place the star bow at the center of the gift for maximum impact.

Angle Variation

Rotate the bow slightly to align with patterns on the wrapping paper or to add dynamic tension.

Coordinating with Wrapping Paper

Solid Colors

Use metallic or glitter star bows on solid-colored paper to let the bow stand out.

Patterned Paper

Select wrapping paper with subtle patterns if using an ornate bow to avoid visual overload.

Adding Ribbons and Bands

Underlay Strips

Wrap the gift with ribbon bands crossing horizontally and vertically before adding the bow.

Contrasting Textures

Use matte ribbons beneath a glitter star bow for contrast.

Variations and Creative Ideas

Multiple Layers

Create additional layers with smaller star bows stacked on top for a 3D effect.

Different Sizes

Make star bows of varying sizes and cluster them together on larger gifts.

Color Themes

Use colors that match holiday themes—red and green for Christmas, blue and silver for a winter motif.

Applications beyond Gift Wrapping

Ornaments

Attach a loop of string to the star bow to hang it as a tree ornament.

Garland Decorations

String multiple star bows together to create a festive garland.

Table Settings

Use star bows as decor on place cards or napkin rings for holiday dinners.

By mastering the star bow, you've added a dazzling and festive design to your bow-making repertoire. This shape captures the wonder of the holidays and can be adapted in countless ways to enhance your seasonal decorations and gifts.

In these chapters, we've explored advanced bow designs that offer endless possibilities for creativity. From the sculptural potential of wired ribbons to the layered complexity of stacked bows, the elegance of flower shapes, and the sparkling allure of star bows, you're now equipped with the knowledge and techniques to create truly remarkable decorations.

As you continue your bow-making journey, remember that experimentation and personal expression are at the heart of crafting. Use these techniques as a foundation, but don't hesitate to innovate and make each creation uniquely yours.

TUTORIAL VIDEOS

How to make a simple single-loop bow

How to Tutorial Tie a perfect bow hack single-sided ribbon cardmaking grosgrain satin Christmas by Sarah Trebilcock

https://www.youtube.com/watch?v=2VcuKkRTZOw

How to make a classic two-loop bow

Easy Double Bow Tutorial Perfect for Wreaths, DIYs, and Home Décor by keeping it Simple

https://www.youtube.com/watch?v=0R2q_BnDYCA

How to make a pom-pom bow

How to Make a Pom Pom Bow and Variations - Step 1

The Container Store

https://www.youtube.com/watch?v=SS7BCrs2xJg

How to make bows with wired ribbon

How to Make a Bow with Wired Ribbon - 5 EASY Ways by Gina Luker

https://www.youtube.com/watch?v=K4prh8tGs0I

How to make layered bows

Three-Layer Elegance in 3:33 Create Stunning Three-Layered Hair Bows Effortless **by Anjurisa**

https://www.youtube.com/watch?v=BJRX27cViaA

How to make a flower-shaped bow

Floral Arrangements: How to Make Floral Bows by **ehowgarden**

https://www.youtube.com/watch?v=0n-ZJolJydo

How to make a star bow with a ribbon

DIY, How to Make Star Bow, Ribbon Art (111) **by WRAPSIR**

https://www.youtube.com/watch?v=gtPBo3Af1xI

Printed in Dunstable, United Kingdom